Prepper Comms

A Practical Guide to Radio Communications for the
Bushcraft, Prepper and Wild Camping Community

Paul Gledhill

© Paul Gledhill 2018

Thanks.
Bethany & Kerry for your support.
WBO for your friendship.

FOREWORD	6
BIOGRAPHY	8
INTRODUCTION	9
WHY ARE COMMS IMPORTANT?	13
SITUATIONS	16
WHAT YOU NEED TO KNOW	18
OPERATIONAL SECURITY (OPSEC)	23
REPEATERS	25
MORE THINGS TO KNOW	27
RADIOS	31
LPD433	34
OTHER TYPES OF RADIO	36
Scanners	36
Digital Radios.	37
ACCESSORIES	38

CONNECTORS	39
CABLES	43
PROGRAMMING RADIOS	45
ANTENNAS	54
MAKE YOUR OWN PORTABLE ANTENNA	57
HOW TO BECOME A RADIO HAM	69
THE GO BAG	72
RAYNET	76
EMERGENCY PROCEDURES	77
The Listening Watch	77
The Call Down System	78
EMP HARDENING	81
Causes of EMP	81
The effects of EMP	83
Preparation for EMP	85
Make A Faraday Cage	86

Glossary of Terms	88
FREQUENCY TABLES	**90**
PMR	90
Citizens Band (CB)	92
Ham	95
2 Metre Band	96
70CM Band	101
Marine Band	106
Air Band	111
PHONETIC ALPHABET	**123**
MORSE CODE	**124**
CONTACT	**125**
HAM RADIO TRAINING	**126**

Foreword

It wasn't something that I ever planned to do, but writing this book has filled a gap. I took up Wild Camping in 2017 and thoroughly loved it. There is a crossover here between the world of camping, prepping, Survivalism and Bushcraft.

I looked for a book that already did this, but what I found were almost entirely American and of little practical use to those in the British Isles.

I don't profess to be the expert in Survival or Prepping, but I have worked my entire life in radio. Whether it be in the broadcast medium, or my 8-year stint in the Royal Air Force as a communications technician.

What I saw when I entered the scene was interesting. An eclectic mix of people who want to be away from the world for a while but at the same time needing to remain in touch with it. Or those who are concerned at the route that civilization is taking and doubts about how long it may last.

It set me thinking about the possibilities that radio has for these 'groups'. For the prepper, reliance on mobile phones is a non-starter. For the bushcrafter and the wild camper, a means of staying in touch with others. Whether the group has split to forage for firewood, or they are camping out of sight. Safety and medical considerations could require comms, but the phone is off. Also, simply put, many of the places where they go are simply off grid and away from cellular phone masts.

Radios are a no brainer but, to someone without my background, they are a thing of mystery. A radio is essential to every person who takes up these pursuits. As important as knowing how to start a fire or to tie a knot.

People of all sorts come to this from all walks of life. I have purposefully stayed away from politics and conspiracies. I seek only to educate.

Enjoy this book and find it useful. I always welcome your feedback and suggestions.

Many thanks,

Paul Gledhill (G7BHE / EI6HOB)
Co. Kerry, Ireland. Jan 2018.

Biography

Paul is a UK based Radio Presenter, Podcaster, Voice Over Artist and Amateur Radio Operator. He started his career in offshore radio before moving on to Independent Local Radio in England and the Channel Islands.

Becoming a Radio Ham at the age of 16, he obtained a good grounding in communications before eventually joining the Royal Air Force as a Telecommunications Technician.

A fan of wild camping, Bushcraft and prepping, he recognised early on that there was a need for a conversation in these communities about enhancing themselves with radio communications ability.

A dedicated 80's fan, you may just catch his radio show Gledders 80's MixTape from time to time on HCR104fm.

Introduction

In this book, I will be showing you why you need communications, explain your options, show you how to get started and most importantly, I will be giving you lots of vital information in order to understand radio communication.

The terms 'Prepper' and 'Radio Ham' often have negative connotations amongst society. Seen as a little whacky and members of the 'tin foil hat' brigade, they are sometimes ridiculed and not taken seriously.

Society is unfortunately doing itself a disservice. Because both groups have knowledge that will prove invaluable should an event occur that causes the communications system to fail.

This guide aims to be practical and above all informative

What is Prepping?

Ask yourself these questions. Do you keep matches and candles in a drawer somewhere? Do you have a torch with batteries stored at home and in the car? The chances are you answered yes to both of these questions and that makes you a Prepper.

The dictionary on my iPad describes a Prepper this way:

prepper

ˈprɛpə/

noun NORTH AMERICAN

noun: **prepper**; plural noun: **preppers**

1. a person who believes a catastrophic disaster or emergency is likely to occur in the future and makes active preparations for it, typically by stockpiling food, ammunition, and other supplies. "there's no agreement among preppers about what disaster is most imminent"

I disagree with the use of the word 'catastrophic' in this definition. Also, as this is designed for the UK readership, you are unlikely to be stockpiling ammunition either.

Granted, many Preppers are waiting for 'The Big One'. But to be a Prepper, you only have to be prepared. It's the old Cub Scout motto, Be Prepared. I'm not convinced that Lord Baden-Powell was waiting for Armageddon. He was surely thinking of practical solutions to surmountable problems.

The Prepper community is as varied as it is large. On the basic level, there is the home owner who has the candles for power cuts, or a few extra tins in case they catch a cold. At the other extreme you have organised groups with converted missile silos and years of supplies.

I am making an assumption that you are not at that end of the scale, but if you are, it's nice to have you along for the ride, please save me a bunk.

In its most basic form, Prepping is simply being prepared for something that may occur. Insurance, if you like. Preppers often prepare for the known rather than the unknown.

To me, a Prepper is a person who simply identifies a potential situation and then creates a solution that will either correct it or allow them to easier deal with it.

The choice of how much prepping you do is simply one for you. No two Preppers are the same. Each has their limit or belief of what to prep for. But beware, prepping can be addictive and time consuming.

In the past, Preppers have had a bad reputation. Admittedly there are some 'interesting' characters who get involved. But the majority are just normal everyday folk. However, the media would have you think they are all crazy or paranoid.

As with any problem, the best way to deal with it is a common sense, logical approach. One that is practical and as straight forward as possible.

What is required is a logical and methodical approach to an issue. This book aims to give you exactly that.

In a bit, we will be looking at some situations that have occurred in the UK and further afield.

Why are comms important?

For thousands of years, humans managed to chug along without the aid of electronic communication methods. But you can't un-invent them now they are here. We have become used to switching on a radio in the car, to watching the TV at home and to accessing the internet virtually everywhere.

To say that communications are an everyday part of our lives is to state the obvious. Phoning your mother to check she is ok without driving to the next town, ordering pizza from an app on your phone, online banking. All of these things require you to be able to operate and maintain some sort of communications device.

We have grown to rely on communications and when they go, the pains really start to come on. Modern day communications rely on a network of hubs to keep going. The idea of hubs is that they are survivable, if one goes down, another takes over. Or we would hope so.

All of your local emergency services and the national government require a robust communications system. Yet everything is done on a budget. When you cut costs, someone is often cutting a corner. We have all heard of IT projects that have cost billions and never came to fruition. The early days of the British telephone system were calamitous. Need quickly outpaced ability and you started to find that more than one household were sharing a telephone line. This is where the phrase 'Party Line' comes from.

Advances in telephone communications came on rapidly in the intervening years and the use of landlines has decreased significantly. When was the last time you saw someone using a telephone box for making a call?

Rapidly progressing through the age of pagers, one-way telephones and onto cellular phones we have now arrived at a stage where the modern phone is a GPS, a computer, a camera, a games console and you can even make a call on it.

These telephone networks rely on the ability to provide them with electricity. When that electricity goes, their backups will rapidly deplete. Bit by bit the communications system will collapse.

This might sound dramatic. But recently, in the small town where I live, some enterprising thieves decided to dig up the road and steal a lot of copper cabling. Unfortunately, that cabling was the main pipeline for telephone and internet into the town. For two weeks, we were without landline phones and the ability to use the internet at home.

You may think that it's easy to continue in these circumstances by using mobile phones. But the cell system rapidly became overrun. Ambulances, the Police and Fire Brigade had to rely on radios. Local businesses were cut off from their customers. The financial loss was huge. This was even before you try to think of the myriad ways that someone could be inconvenienced. You are running late getting home from work, the kids are still at nursery and you are unable to contact the staff. It goes on.

Situations

1928 The Thames River in London became flooded. Thankfully the loss of life was fairly low at 14 but thousands were made homeless.

1953 Severe flooding hit the east coast of England. 307 people lost their lives.

1987 The south east of England was hit by an unexpected hurricane. Swathes of Essex lost comms as the telephone system went down. The winds drove water over sea walls onto low lying areas and interrupted the power to homes. Something in the region of 15 million trees were felled, causing disruption to the transport network, electricity supplies and the telephone system.

2005 Hurricane Katrina hit New Orleans. It was responsible for the deaths of over 1300 people and the rending homeless of hundreds of thousands. Some areas of New Orleans are still in ruins. Social structures entirely failed. Police were seen looting supermarkets. It was days before help began to arrive.

2006 A brief Tornado touched down in London. Mercifully only one person received injuries but damage totalled in millions of pounds.

2007 Floods hit Gloucestershire. 13 dead. All rail closed, many roads were shut and over 400,000 were left without drinking water.

This is just a very small number of incidents compared to the real list of what has occurred in living memory. As you can see, each and every one of the incidents listed above it a natural disaster. The assumption that Preppers are waiting for nuclear war or volcanoes spilling forth molten lava may be relevant for some parts of the world but the UK perspective is somewhat different.

Let's be honest with ourselves, in the event of a nuclear strike on the UK we have pretty much had it. We can be concerned about the EMP (Electro-Magnetic Pulse) of an air burst nuke over the British Isles, but the vast majority won't live to tell the tale. That's not to say we shouldn't be planning for other causes of EMP and we will come on to that.

Let's take an idiots guide through radio communications and give you a whole bunch of stuff you need to know.

What You Need To Know

Radio signals travel in waves. The higher the frequency, the shorter the antenna. To some extent the higher the frequency, the shorter the distance it will travel. That is not a hard and fast rule but some of the later chapters will explain for you.

For the purpose of this guide we are going to be focusing on frequencies in the VHF and UHF spectrum.

VHF (Very High Frequency) is a section of the spectrum between 30 MHz and 300 MHz
UHF (Ultra High Frequency) another section of the spectrum between 300MHz and 3 GHz

That's a lot of MHz's I hear you say, but what does it mean?

Look at the image below. Another way of saying Hz is cycles. In old movies, you might hear people talking about Kilocycles or Megacycles. This is the same as Kilohertz and MegaHertz. (KHz & MHz).

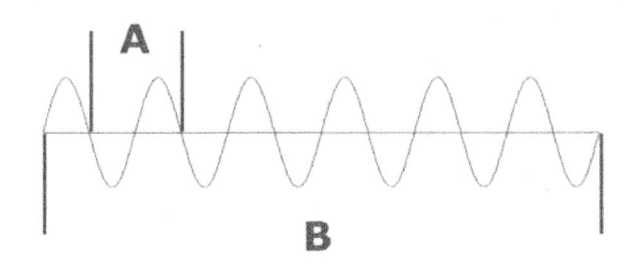

The distance covered between the top of one peak to the next is a cycle, or a wavelength. In the image, you see that 'A' marks the midway point of one downward slope to the midway point of the next downward slope. This is also a cycle. It doesn't really matter which part you start at as long as you know that a cycle is simply the corresponding point on the next wave.

'B' represents Frequency. Let's say that the two sticks indicate one second has passed.
You can see that the image above represents 6 cycles per second, or 6 Hertz (6Hz)

Heinrich Hertz was a German boffin who proved the existence of electromagnetic waves, this was named after him.

In radio terms, you will be dealing with MegaHertz quite a lot. 1 MegaHertz is 1 million cycles per second.

So, you can write a frequency more than one way.

1,000,000 Hz is exactly the same as 1 MHz.

Drawing 1 million cycles above might just have been a little awkward.

GigaHertz on the other hand means billion cycles per second. This is a much higher rate. Radios do operate at these frequencies and so do microwave ovens. That's why you see ovens rated in Watts. It is radio transmitter in a box. The radio waves make the water molecules in your food move really quickly and the resultant friction creates heat.

You may hear people referring to Megs and Gigs. That might confuse you, as you probably use the same terminology when talking about computers.

There are other wave bands which you can be aware of, Long Wave for instance, once used by radio stations for mostly voice programs. Shortwave, once popular for broadcasters who wanted to get their signals around the world. Music programs were broadcast on Shortwave, but frankly the audio quality was not good. A good use of Shortwave by governments is the mysterious Numbers Station. Often, this would be a curious program broadcast after the official broadcaster had gone off the air. A current user of this system is North Korea. It is used generally to send coded messages to operatives in other countries. The internet put an end to most of them, but you can probably understand why North Korea still use it.

You probably know Medium Wave already, it's still in use for radio programs across much of the world. Not very good but usable for music, but when night comes it is often very poor due to interference from other stations on the same frequency.

One thing you may remember about Medium Wave is how it changes as night. In fact, in some parts of western Europe, at night you can still hear American stations. Only just, but they are there.

This phenomenon occurs at all frequencies, not just Medium Wave. In fact, at certain times your VHF signals may carry a lot further than you expect.

This is due to something call Propagation. Radiation from the Sun effects the Ionosphere and makes it reflective to radio waves. Your signals from ground level travel in different directions, including upwards. If you have played Pool or Snooker you will be used to the idea of bouncing a ball off a cushion in order to reach farther down the table. Your radio signal bouncing off the Ionosphere is much the same. The level that this occurs at and the times it happens are explained in very scientific ways. They are forecast in much the same way as weather is forecast.

Needless to say, it will happen to you one day and someone from far away will answer your call. It is as thrilling as it is surprising.

Operational Security (OPSEC)

Very few radio systems are secure and you should assume that someone is listening in.

If using Ham Bands and you are licenced, then there is an expectation that you will be using your issued Callsign.

If using PMR, or SHTF has occurred, be very aware that what you say may be intercepted and the information may be used to deprive you of food and equipment. Or worse.

With that in mind, you may wish to not use your names on the radio. Stick to nicknames or self-made callsigns. Use nicknames for places and do not ever say where you live or where you have parked a vehicle.

Avoid referring to what resources you may have.

If mentioning times, have an understanding that the time you give should be plus or minus a set number of minutes or hours.

This does take a bit of discipline if you are part of a group and it is vitally important that all members of it are briefed in and know how to use a radio in an emergency.

Repeaters

Handheld radios and to a lesser extent, mobile radios are limited in range. This is because of a number of factors. Power output and terrain being the most important. A handheld radio putting out 5 watts of radio signal into the atmosphere will suffer from the amount of buildings around it, dense foliage, hills etc.

In order to counter this, Radio Hams have for many years banded together to increase the range of their radios on VHF and UHF by placing repeaters on tall buildings and masts.
Simply put, a repeater will receive a signal and retransmit it.

It's important to note that only licenced Radio Hams have the ability to use these systems. If you are unlicenced and using PMR channels, you will be limited to what you have in your hand.

The next picture is an indicator of how a repeater will assist.

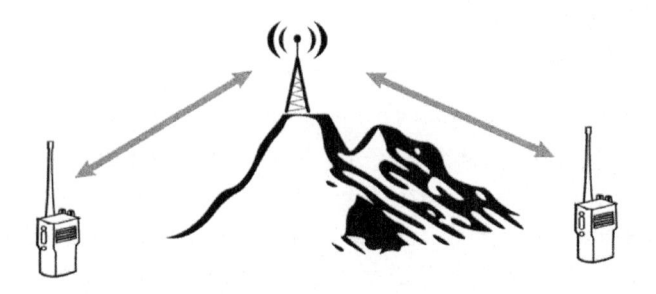

More Things To Know

The type of radio you have in your home or car is known as a *Receiver*. It plucks radio waves out of the air via an *Aerial* or *Antenna*. It then decodes that radio signal and turns it into something you can listen to.

A broadcast radio station has the opposite type of radio. It takes an audio signal, for instance music or speech and converts it into a radio signal. This signal is then sent along a cable to an antenna where it is released into the air. This type of radio is a *Transmitter*

The third type of radio is the one you are going to be learning about in this guide. It is called a *Transceiver*. It does the job of the other two types of radio, but in one box. Transceivers come in all shapes and sizes. Handheld versions are often known as Walkie-Talkies, Handies or Handhelds. Other versions exist for permanent fitting in a vehicle and for desk use.

Every radio needs an *Aerial*. Without one, radio signals are trapped in the radio or in the air. These come in all shapes and sizes. Some are much better than others and we will be looking at some different versions. Aerials are very technical but there are some basics which you absolutely must understand. Thankfully, you don't need to be a boffin to get along with them.

The type of radio you are allowed to use is going to differ dependent upon whether you decide to get a licence or not.

You will probably have seen little radios for sale in camping or electronics shops. These are known as PMR or Private Mobile Radio. They have eight channels and operate at about 446 MHz which is in the UHF band. These are good for a couple of miles or less and the range is very much dependant on what is around you. If you have a clear line of sight to the other radio you will get much further. If you have a lot in the way then your range will be limited.

These radios are perfectly acceptable for Prepper use but you must take into account the limited output power of the signal and other handicaps. For instance, these radios often have an antenna that is far from efficient. Some of the radio signal that the radio puts into it when transmitting will be wasted. Also, you are limited to those 8 channels. You can only use one at a time of course, but if everyone starts using them in an emergency, it can get noisy.

In the UK, PMR radios that you buy from a store do not require a licence. This makes for a cheap and simple form of radio communication. However, these are low power devices which conform to an EU standard. You are limited to a maximum of 0.5 watts.

Another option, which also happens to be my preferred option, is the Amateur transceiver. These are designed and built for hobbyists. They have a whole bunch of benefits over PMR and the prices start in exactly the same region as a PMR radio.

The benefits of this type of radio are in the ability to use different frequencies to PMR, to use more power for transmitting and the facilities provided by the network of repeaters in the UK and around the world.

UK radio hams can also take their radios abroad and use them under reciprocal licensing agreements. I will tell you about licensing in a later section but for now, know that it is well worth it for several reasons.

Comparing the Motorola with the Baofeng. You can pick up a pair of these for virtually the same price.

If you do decide to stay with PMR radios but want a little more power, you can get a business licence. However, I do think it is a needless expense.

On the theme of things you need to know, here's a few more.

Being high up gives you a greater range with your radio.

Being outside gives a better signal than being indoors or in a car.

If you are indoors or in a vehicle, then having an external antenna will be a huge improvement.

It is not possible to remove the antenna on a PMR radio or to connect to an external antenna.

Weather can affect the performance of your radio, both to the good and to the bad.

Keep your battery in tip top condition. If the radio you have allows for it, have a spare antenna and battery.

Always test radios before use and if stored, test them regularly.

Always check that nobody is transmitting before you transmit.

Don't mess about on the radio. Playing music or talking for too long could stop important message traffic and potentially could cause someone not to get assistance.

Have a radio 'Go Bag'. I will go into this later.

Radios

Below you will find a few examples.

The first is a PMR radio, as previously mentioned it is limited to 0.5 watts. It is the licence free system which is handy for basic uses. You cannot remove the antenna to connect to a better one.

These are nice and cheap but you pay way over the odds for the expensive ones as they are the same spec as the super cheap PMR radios.

The second radio is the business variant of PMR. This one is made by Hytera and is very well made. It is also quite pricey. It requires a business licence which is £75 for five years and give you the ability to run handhelds at 5 watts and vehicle mounted radios at 25 watts. Licences are available from Ofcom. www.ofcom.org.uk

The third and fourth units are amateur radio transceivers. The third being a cheap and cheerful unit from Baofeng. This model is capable of an output of 8 watts. At a price of £35 it is definitely one of the cheaper units but definitely not to be discarded. Hams swear by these radios and they have the ability to be programmed to frequencies outside the normal Ham Radio bands. For instance, these can pick up Marine VHF so you can monitor the coastguard and lifeboat. Quite handy in an emergency and cheaper than PMR! It's 8 watts of transmit power is 16 times more powerful than the PMR radio and it can work on those frequencies too. This radio is a Preppers dream, it already has quite a following. Beware, these radios can also transmit on the Marine Frequencies. If you do not have a Marine VHF licence and you transmit on those frequencies, you are breaking the law. But listening is good fun and can be quite handy.

The fourth radio is a Yaesu VX-8DE. Yaesu are a tried and tested Ham Radio manufacturer. They also make commercial units under the brand name 'Vertex'. This radio has numerous memories, a very wide band receive coverage, starting from Shortwave, up through Airband, Marine VHF and the Ham Radio bands. It can even send intermittent data transmissions using a system called APRS. These transmissions are encoded with your call sign and GPS coordinates, which can then be received by others and plotted on an onscreen map. All Gucci stuff but the decision to go this route ought to be part of your 'needs assessment' as it isn't cheap.

Radios five and six are both Citizens Band units. Rising to almost cult status in the late 70's and 80's, CB radio became phenomenally popular. People were meeting up in their cars to show off the equipment and see who could transmit the furthest. Over the years, the popularity has died right down to a level where at my location you can go days without hearing anything. This has positive benefits to the Prepper who will find that the majority of 'annoying' users have moved to PMR. However, there are down sides to CB to. The frequency range they operate in hovers around the 27 MHz mark which place them in the HF band. It is prone to background noise unfortunately and due to the lower frequency, it requires a larger antenna. My experience of handheld CB has not been positive. I'm not suggesting that you discount CB entirely but you may want to do some comparing before parting with your cash.

LPD433

Some of the newer PMR radios also come with a system called LPD433 (Low Powered Devices).

These are available from companies like Intek. For very close communications you could consider this. They were initially decided upon by the European Union due to the sheer level of traffic over PMR radios, which are limited to 8 channels.

LPD radios work in the 70cm band which is mainly used by Radio Hams. It has 69 channels, which sounds great but you are limited to a total of 10 Milliwatts. Compare with Radio Hams who are allowed to use 40 Watts in this band and you will soon realise that this system is very much the poor relation to Ham Radio, but then so is PMR.

Key Fobs for remote entry to vehicles also operate on this band.

Whilst outside the scope of this book, it is worth knowing about other types of radio.

Other types of radio

Scanners

These are receiving only radios that give you the ability to listen on multiple radio frequencies at the same time. The frequencies are all programmed in by you and it constantly scans through them, stopping when something is transmitting. The use of scanners is a popular hobby in itself and many Facebook groups exist to support owners. One of the best is National UK Scanning (NUKS).

Digital Radios.

Not the same as the DAB you may have in your kitchen. These radios convert your voice into a digital signal that is then transmitted. It is decoded by the other radios in your group. The benefit of these is in the signal quality. The audio is often unnervingly clear. There is a downside though. If you are on the fringe of a signal you will find that receiving the audio is a hit and miss affair. Where a normal radio will be much more forgiving. You will suddenly find the signal dropping out. Hams call this the R2D2 effect. There are scanners that can monitor digital radios. Like the radios themselves, these scanners are more expensive. If you do use these radios you will find they are less likely to be intercepted by others. At the time of writing, these radios come in three different flavours. DMR (Digital Mobile Radio) is based on the business radios made by Motorola. DSTAR, Made by Icom predominantly, although Kenwood have made one also. Finally, Fusion by Yaesu. This is the new kid on the block, Digital radios have some great features, including GPS and the ability to send pictures. But you must very carefully decide what it is that you want before you splash the cash.

Accessories

As with all radios, there are accessories to have. It's always a good idea to have a case to protect it, spare battery, car charger, mains charger and a replacement antenna. On top of this, you may wish to invest some time in making a deployable antenna that can be hoisted up a tree to give you a much improved transmit and receive. Instructions can be found later in this book.

Most, if not all, variants of radio have the ability to connect an external speaker/microphone.

Antenna connectors vary with Ham Radio kit. You should be aware of what connector goes with what radio. The type of connector is what you would ask for if replacing the antenna.

Almost without fail, radios come with the standard 'rubber duck' type of antenna. Generally, these are rubbish. It is always worth buying another. Consider antennas by companies like Watson, Diamond or Nagoya. They are available for each type of radio with the exception of PMR.

Connectors

BNC Socket   **BNC Plug**

BNC
Found on older Ham Radio equipment and is a standard fit on most radio scanners. Also found on a wide variety of test equipment. It's a relatively easy plug to fit.

SMA Male

SMA Male

In use on handheld radios made by the majority of 'big name' radio manufacturers like, Yaesu, Kenwood and Icom.

SMA Female

SMA Female

For some reason, the cheaper Chinese radios went for this version on their radios. Basically, it is exactly the opposite of the radios above. This can cause some confusion when buying antennas over eBay or Amazon, so make sure you order the right one.

SO239 Socket    **PL259 Plug**

SO239
Not usually found on handheld radios. These would normally be located on the rear of mobile and desktop units. SO239 is a socket. The plug is called a PL259 and it is very easy to fit.

Antenna Adaptors

| SMA Female to SO239 | SMA Male to SO239 | SMA Female to BNC | SMA Male to BNC |

A must, if you own one of these radios is to have a collection of antenna adaptors. The most common are shown here. There are many more available via www.hamgoodies.co.uk and eBay.

SMA Female to SO239
Allows connection between Baofeng and Pofung Chinese Radios and an antenna that has a PL259 plug.

SMA Male to SO239
Allows connection between Yaesu, Icom and Kenwood radios and antennas with a PL259 plug.

SMA Female to BNC

Allows connection between Baofeng and Pofung type Chinese Radio with an antenna with a BNC connector.

SMA Male to BNC
Connecting the big-name radio, Yaesu, Icom and Kenwood with antennas that have a PL259 plug.

Cables

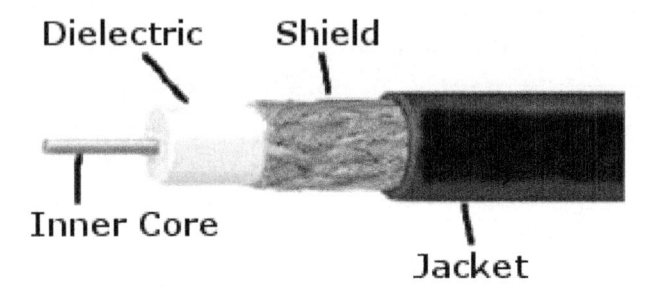

Dielectric, Shield, Inner Core, Jacket

Coaxial Cable is the link between a radio and an external antenna. It is the stuff of legend and mystery. Many radio hams can be found frothing at the mouth over this subject. But to make it easy, the most common antenna cable you will come across for radio use is called RG58. It has an impedance of 50 Ohms. You don't need to worry about impedance too much, as long as you are using the right stuff. Coax, as it is better known, consists of a copper core made of one or more strands. This carries the radio signal from the radio to the antenna and vice versa. Around this copper core is a rubbery plastic protector called a dielectric. This provides protection and insulation for the internal core. Running along the outside of the dielectric is a further set of copper strands in a mesh pattern. This provides shielding from interference and also prevents the internal core from radiating radio signals, thus becoming an antenna itself. Coaxial cable is waterproof but it also needs to be cared for as it can have chunks taken out of it when closed in doors or windows.

It available by the metre or on 50/100 metre drums from shops like Maplin.

The other types of cable you will come across are chargers, just like with a mobile phone. The next similar cable is the USB cable which you can buy to program radios from a computer.

Programming Radios

Programming radios can be done in 2 main ways. The first and most effective way is by the use of a computer and a USB cable. There is a free program called CHIRP which can be used to program many of the Yaesu and cheaper Chinese radios.

Be aware though that you cannot program the cheaper PMR radios or any of the CB radios.

Another programming software is made by RT System, an American company but widely sold in Ham Radio stores in the UK, as well as from RT Systems own website. I am a big fan of their software. It does cost and sometimes you need a special cable which is also available from them, but the ease of use is undeniable.

The last way of programming a radio is not necessarily available on each different type. Many but not all can be programmed through a keypad on the front. With the Baofeng this is a huge faff and I would recommend using CHIRP.

So, what do you need to know when programming a radio?

The frequency you want to receive on.

The frequency you want to transmit on.
Any offset frequency.
Whether you need a CTCSS tone.
What you are going to call that channel in the memories.
Power setting

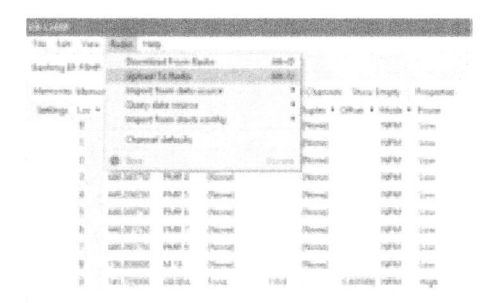

If for instance you are going to program a PMR frequency then it is very simple.

The frequency for channel 1 of PMR is 446.00625 MHz
It is a simplex channel, which means you transmit and receive on the same frequency
No CTCSS tone is required.

In this example, we are going to use CHIRP to program a Baofeng radio to use the PMR frequencies. I have also added 2 others, the first being the Marine Emergency Channel 16 and the last being the details you need to access the Amateur Radio Repeater GB3DA. That is the call sign of a repeater based in Essex.

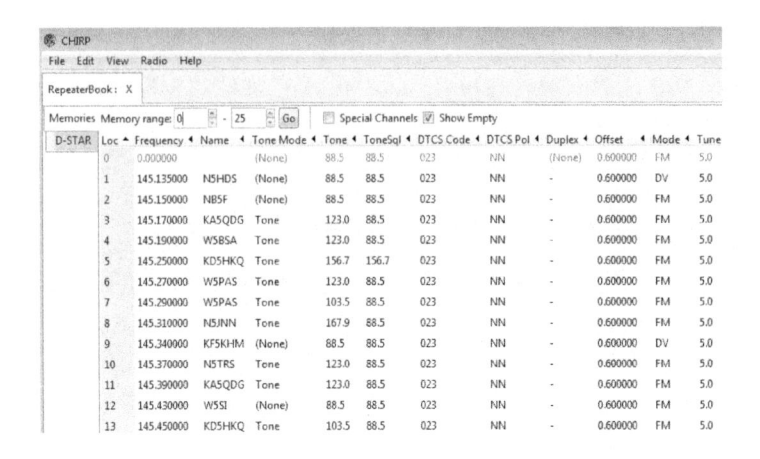

D-STAR	Loc	Frequency	Name	Tone Mode	Tone	ToneSql	DTCS Code	DTCS Pol	Duplex	Offset	Mode	Tune
	0	0.000000		(None)	88.5	88.5	023	NN	(None)	0.600000	FM	5.0
	1	145.135000	N5HDS	(None)	88.5	88.5	023	NN	-	0.600000	DV	5.0
	2	145.150000	NB5F	(None)	88.5	88.5	023	NN	-	0.600000	FM	5.0
	3	145.170000	KA5QDG	Tone	123.0	88.5	023	NN	-	0.600000	FM	5.0
	4	145.190000	W5BSA	Tone	123.0	88.5	023	NN	-	0.600000	FM	5.0
	5	145.250000	KD5HKQ	Tone	156.7	156.7	023	NN	-	0.600000	FM	5.0
	6	145.270000	W5PAS	Tone	123.0	88.5	023	NN	-	0.600000	FM	5.0
	7	145.290000	W5PAS	Tone	103.5	88.5	023	NN	-	0.600000	FM	5.0
	8	145.310000	N5JNN	Tone	167.9	88.5	023	NN	-	0.600000	FM	5.0
	9	145.340000	KF5KHM	(None)	88.5	88.5	023	NN	-	0.600000	DV	5.0
	10	145.370000	N5TRS	Tone	123.0	88.5	023	NN	-	0.600000	FM	5.0
	11	145.390000	KA5QDG	Tone	123.0	88.5	023	NN	-	0.600000	FM	5.0
	12	145.430000	W5SI	(None)	88.5	88.5	023	NN	-	0.600000	FM	5.0
	13	145.450000	KD5HKQ	Tone	103.5	88.5	023	NN	-	0.600000	FM	5.0

Using CHIRP is easy but there are a couple of things you need to do before using it.

Go to the website and download the software. www.chirp.danplanet.com

Install it

Plug your USB programming cable in
Makes sure that Windows recognises the cable and assigns a port to it. You will find this in the Device Manager in Windows. Depending on what cable and what version of Windows, you may have to install a driver. My experience has found that cables that include a PL2303 chip are not as good as cables with an FTDI chip. Windows seems to like the FTDI more.

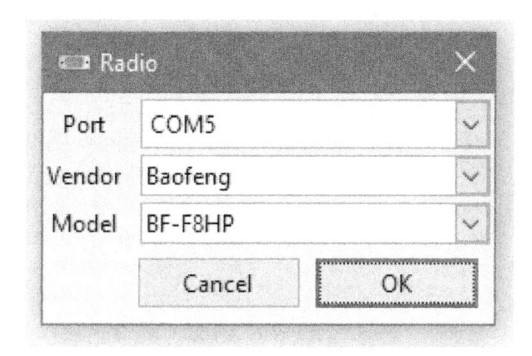

Plug your radio in and choose 'Download from Radio'.

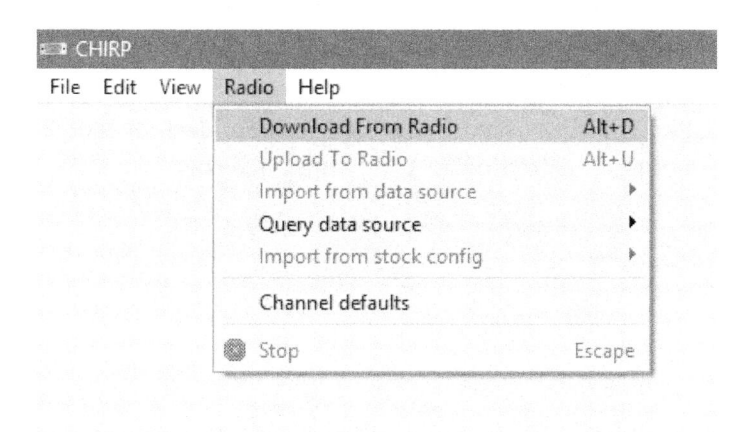

Assuming you have all the settings right, you should see this…

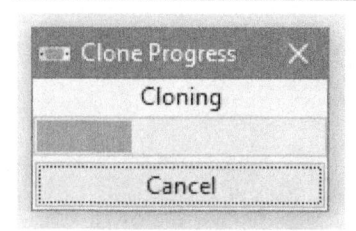

This will create a screen within CHIRP that contains all of the information that is in the radio. It also has the benefit of creating a file with all of the correct settings. This is important when you come to uploading your work back into the radio. If your radio is brand new then you may have very little, if any, information on the CHIRP screen.

Once you have your config downloaded onto the screen, you should see something like this.

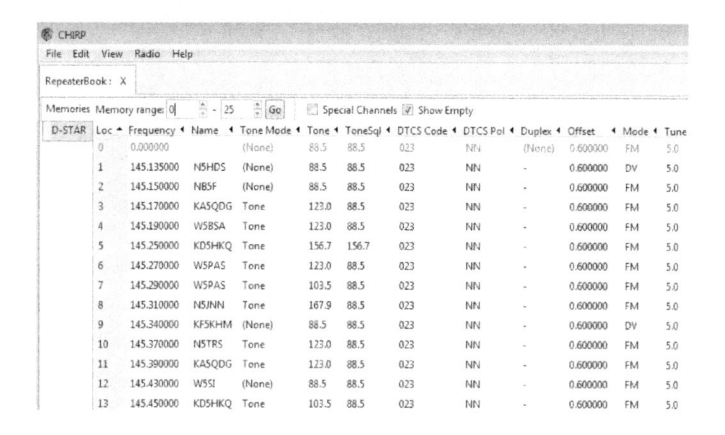

If you have bought a Baofeng radio, you may find that there are a whole bunch of channels programmed in already, much like the image above. In the UK, it is unlikely that you are allowed to use any of the frequencies listed. So, you really do need to delete the rubbish and program in your own.

CHIRP BLANK CONFIG

Let's go to line 0 and enter the following.

Transmit Frequency 446.00625
Receive Frequency 446.00625
Offset 0
CTCSS Blank
Name PMR 1
TX Power Low

You have now successfully created the first programmed channel.
Using the same method and the frequency lists at the back you can now go through and program the other 7 PMR channels. (Frequencies in the back of this book).

Using the frequency reference again we can see that the frequency for the Marine Emergency Channel 16 is 156.800 MHz

The same setting as above will need to be filled in for that memory channel. However, make sure that Transmit and Receive are the same and use the name Marine 16. This will enable you to monitor Lifeboat and Coastguard radio traffic.

Let's look at the settings for using a British ham radio repeater.

The settings for the GB3DA memory channel are different. Because repeaters work in a different way.

To access this repeater, you would need to enter

Receive Frequency 145.725
Transmit Frequency 145.125
Offset -0.600
CTCSS 110.9
Name GB3DA
Power High

OK, you are now dying to know what CTCSS is and why we need an offset for repeaters.

Let's tackle the Offset first.

Repeaters do literally that. They repeat your transmission for others to hear, but they do it in real time. So, taking the above example, you are monitoring the output of GB3DA on 145.725 when you decide to talk. So, you press and hold the transmit button on the radio and begin speaking. Your radio knows it is a repeater and transmits 0.6 MHz lower than the main repeater frequency, IE 145.125 MHz. By doing this, the repeater is able to listen to your signal and retransmit it in real time to everyone else. Then when you finish talking, your radio automatically goes back to the main frequency. When someone else transmits, their radio does what yours did and you are able to hear them in real time too. The benefit of this is that you may be out of rage of another handheld radio, but as long as you can both access the repeater you can hear each other.

On to CTCSS. Continuous Tone-Coded Squelch System.

If a repeater retransmitted everything that it heard on its input frequency, everyone would be listening to a lot of hiss, crackle and static that naturally floats around on radio frequencies. That would rapidly become annoying.

The people who run repeaters have a special way of allowing you access whilst blocking interference. They set their repeater to listen for a subtle tone and as long as that accompanies a signal it will retransmit... or repeat.

They publish the tone frequency for each repeater and if you don't program it in, it won't work.

GB3DA has an access tone of 110.9 Hz. When you transmit and it hears that tone, you are in business. Get the tone setting wrong, or leave it blank, it won't retransmit your signal. Other repeaters may have tones of different values.

CTCSS can also be used on simplex frequencies. At times where you may have other people nearby and using the same frequencies, setting CTCSS on all radios in your net could be a real bonus. Whilst your radio would receive all signals on a frequency, it filters out the ones that don't have your CTCSS setting and you won't be hearing too much rubbish.

The downside to this, is that the other signals can still interfere with the one you want to receive and could potentially block the weaker signal that you are hoping to listen to. It's a bit like two people having a door key each, only one of them is going to fit.

Antennas

No one subject will cause as much debate amongst radio people as the topic of antennas.

There are some very important things to know about them and it would be helpful if you can have a basic understanding.

The perfect antenna is one that is tuned to the frequency that the radio is trying to operate on.

Each frequency has its own wavelength. The wavelength is what defines how long an antenna should be.

So, for instance the antenna length for the 2-meter Ham Band is... wait for it.... 2 meters.

The length for the 70cm Ham Band is 70cm. The 80 Meter band? 80 Meters and so on.

The higher a frequency, the lower the wavelength and vice versa. Antennas at VHF, UHF and SHF frequencies are significantly shorter than for low frequencies. In fact, submarines and trans-Atlantic aircraft still make use of very low frequency radios and they play out a long antenna behind the craft or vessel.

Now the reality is that antennas are not made in these ideal lengths. Everything to do with them is a compromise.

An antenna tuned to 145.500 MHz, also needs to work at 144 and 146. This is known as the wideband property of an antenna.

Handheld radios are normally provided with a small 'rubber duck' antenna. These are generally highly inefficient and a replacement antenna can make a huge difference.

Standard types of antenna are the 'Half Wave', 'Quarter Wave', 'Five Eighths Wave' there are numerous others.

You will notice that the antennas on handheld radios are significantly shorter than the appropriate wavelength. That is because the physical length of the 'rubber duck' hides a little trick. Inside the antenna is a spring or wound cable. If this were stretched out, you should find it to be the correct length.

A really fantastic antenna for the Prepper to have access to is known as a Slim Jim. It isn't the sort of antenna that you are going to walk around with connected to the radio. But for being in position at a camp or for use at home it is highly effective and easy to use.

The portable Slim Jim is made of twin feeder cable, also known as ladder line. This cable is widely available from Ham Radio suppliers. The other good bit of news is that making one for the 2-meter band will save you having to make one for 70 cm's as it works well on both.

Coming off the bottom of the Slim Jim is a length of RG58 coax which is then terminated to the correct connector for your radio.

The top of the antenna can be fixed in lots of different ways, but one very important thing is that you don't want to connect it to metal.

Many Hams and Preppers use a length of Para Cord slung over a tree to hoist the antenna up. Having one of these in your radio Go Bag can make all the difference.

I am going to show you how to make a Slim Jim:

Make Your Own Portable Antenna

Slim Jim Antenna

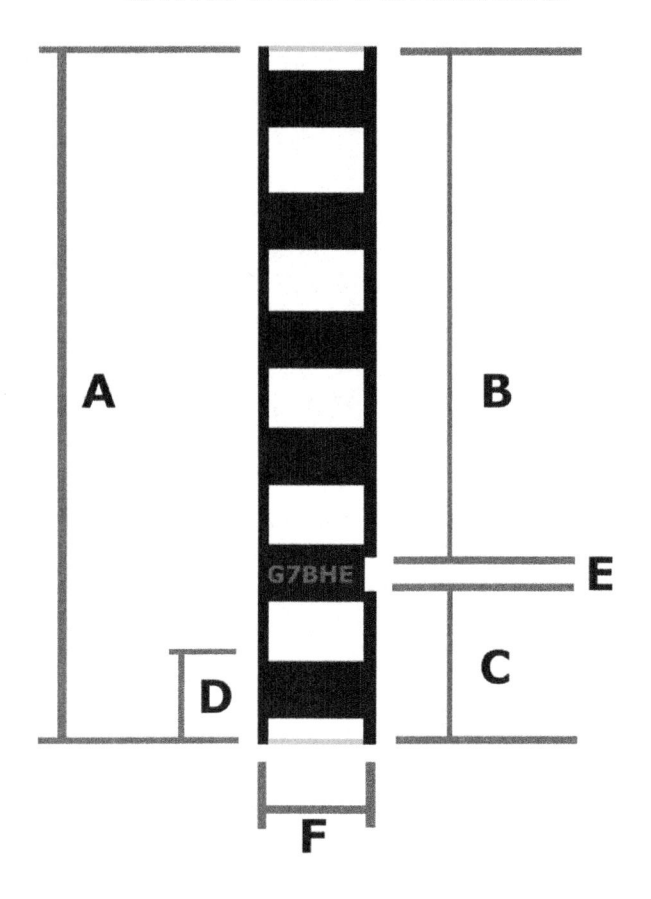

First things first, here is a list of parts you will need.

2 Metres of 300 or 450 Ohm Ladder Line Cable
A length of 50 Ohm RG58 Coaxial Cable
An antenna connector
Clip On Ferrite (Optional)

You will also need:
Sharp Knife
Soldering Iron
Solder

You will need to decide what frequencies your Slim Jim is going to operate at. I am assuming that you are going to be aiming for the 2 Metre Ham Band, IE 144-146MHz.

If you choose to go for other frequencies, (For Instance PMR) then you should consult a Slim Jim Calculator which can be found online with a quick Google search. There is a good one on the M0UKD website.

DOUBLE CHECK YOUR MEASUREMENTS. THESE IMAGES ARE NOT TO SCALE.

Step 1

Using this image as a guide, cut your ladder line cable longer than you need. This is because you need to solder both side together at each end.

Measure along point A. 151cm. Mark off that measurement choosing to move up or down slightly as you wish, so that the other steps will be easier.

Mark off again 2cm above the top mark and 2cm below the bottom mark.

Using some pliers, snip the cable at the furthest marks.

Now bare 2cm of the inner wire at the top and the bottom of both sides.

If you have done this correctly, the black insulator should still be 151cm long.
Now fold the bared inners towards each other and solder together.

Lay out the cable in front of you so that the bottom is nearest and the top farthest away.

On the RIGHT-HAND SIDE ONLY, measure up from the bottom 49.7cm. Mark it off.

Now measure a further 2cm and mark again. This gives you point E.

Using pliers, remove E. It's a simple snip of 2cm.

This will leave you with a gap between B and C. This gap is very important.

For this antenna, the width of point F does not matter.

Step 2

You're now going to create notches, one on either side. This is so that you can solder the coaxial cable to the antenna.

You now need to measure from the bottom and mark at 5cm's (D) on each side.

Do NOT snip.

Using a sharp knife, remove the insulator on each side for a couple of mm's either side of the mark.

Be very careful not to damage the inner conductor or you might cause it to become weak.

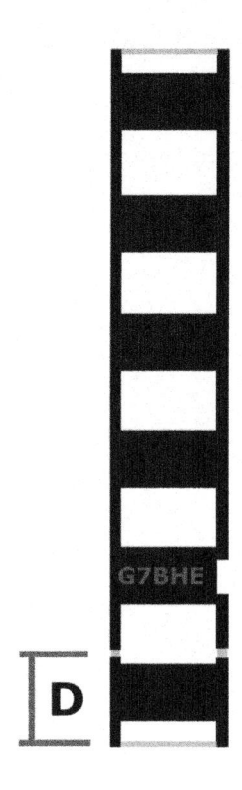

Step 3

Again, using a sharp knife, trim around the outer jacket of one end of the RG58 Coax. About 5 CM should be enough. Try not to damage the fragile shielding strands underneath the outer jacket.

Once you have done that, you may need to gently slice lengthways in order to remove that 5cm section.

You will now be left with 5cm of shielding and inside that 5cm of dielectric.

Pull the shielding to one side and twist it together, in order to expose the dielectric.

Then about 1.5cm up towards the end, use the knife again to gently cut through the dielectric. DO NOT damage the inner core.

Once that is done, gently slide the dielectric off the inner core. You should be left with something that looks like this:

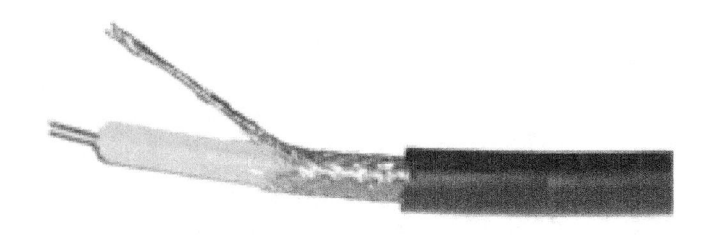

Now that is done you need to solder the inner core to the left-hand notch and the braided shield to the right-hand notch.

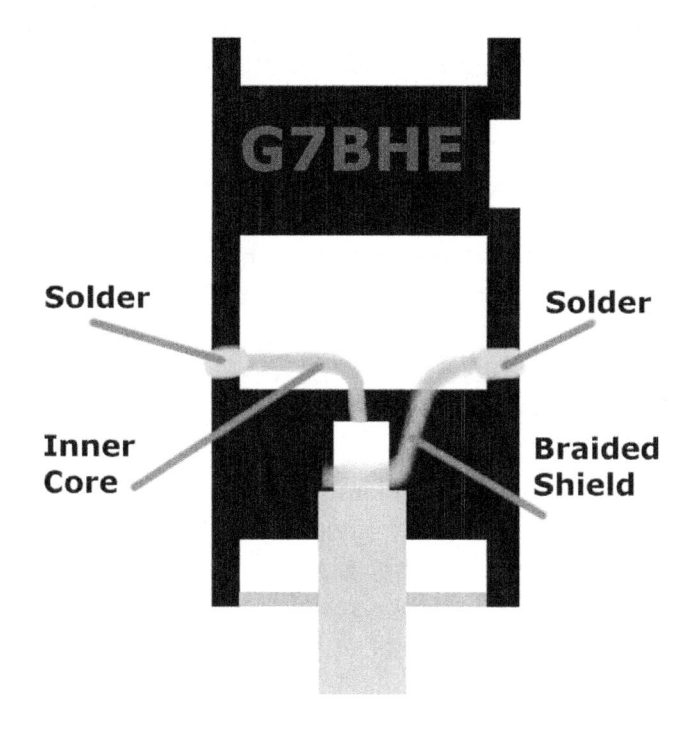

OK this is really coming together now.

You really need to start thinking about practicalities. Using either electrical tape or heat shrink, cover up the lower part of the antenna.

There are two reasons for this. The first is weatherproofing. The second, structural integrity. The coax needs to be held tightly so that the weight of the cable is supported. Also, it prevents undue stresses on the points where the coax connects to the antenna.

At the top of the antenna, consider covering the bare copper with tape. Also, you need a method to hang the antenna. In this image, I have made a hole through one of the plastic crossbars.

Please note, do not hang the antenna on or against metal. In fact, it is good to keep the antenna at least a Quarter Wave away from any metal. That can affect some of the electrical properties and may cause the antenna to operate incorrectly. See the Glossary later in this book under VSWR. Tie Paracord through the hole and hoist it up so that it hangs from a branch for best results.

Finally, you will have something looking like this. Remember, the images are not to scale.

The last thing is to terminate the Coax cable with a suitable connector to allow you attach to your radio.

Personally, I use PL259 plugs in combination with an adapter. Many other Hams use BNC connectors with an adapter. This really is a matter of personal preference. The PL259 is very easy to fit. Below is the antenna made by Pete M0PSX, he chose a BNC connector.

What's that lump just under his thumb? Going back to the list of parts, you will see an optional clip on ferrite. This assists with interference and for the cost of a couple of pounds, it is worth it.

Buy them from www.hamgoodies.co.uk

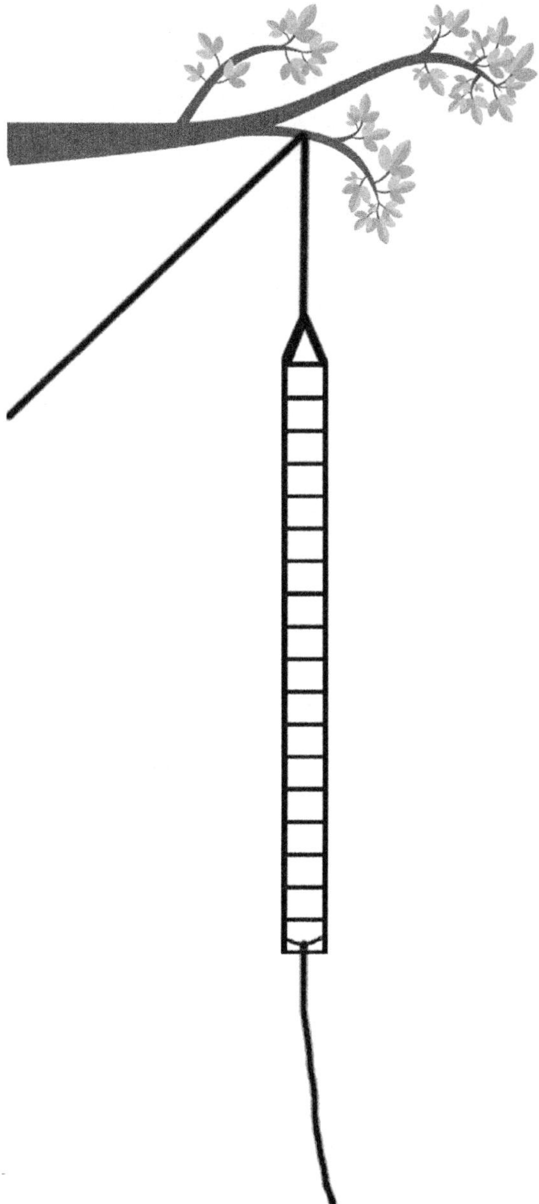

It is vital that you ensure that water does not get into any antenna connector. If it does, it can cause shorting and may result in damage to your radio.

Good use of heat shrink or amalgamating tape can weather proof connectors, providing some protection.

How to Become a Radio Ham

The UK used to have some very strict rules on how to become a Ham. When I took my test, it involved spending a year at Evening Classes learning some very dry theory and practices. I persevered and passed first time, not everyone was so lucky. It was a time consuming and mentally challenging process.

These days, the powers that be have decided that the Ham Radio licence can be obtained at three different levels. "Foundation', 'Intermediate' and 'Full'.

Depending on what level you go in at, you will be issued with a call sign that reflects the level of licence you have achieved.

The vast majority take Foundation first. It requires a much lower level of study and some basic practical knowledge. This is all that is required to get you on the air with a shiny new call sign that begins M6.

Intermediate licence holders call signs begin 2E0 or 2E1 and Full licence holders get an M0.

Older Hams, which sadly I am now one, had callsigns that began with a 'G'. Mine starts G7.

Study for the Foundation exam does not have to be difficult and you can sign up for an online course with Ham Train. The course is completely **free** and in three weeks you will know all you need to know.

In addition to the knowledge side of things, you will need to sit a brief practical session with a qualified assessor. These are often provided by Ham Radio clubs all over the UK for a very small fee.

Ham Train is run by a dedicated Radio Ham, Pete Sipple M0PSX. He is also the force behind the excellent online radio club Essex Ham.

Pete provides handouts, videos and other resources for the beginner and with his course you will be very well prepared to take the exam.

See information on last page.

Some useful links for you:

Essex Ham - www.essexham.co.uk
Ham Train - www.hamtrain.co.uk
Radio Society of Great Britain - www.rsgb.org

Once you have your licence, keeping it is free. All you have to do is revalidate your details every five years.

I really hope that you sign up for Pete's free course and that you join the Ham Radio community. The sheer level of knowledge and assistance that hams can give you is overwhelming. It is a very friendly hobby and there are many different branches of the pastime that you would never get bored with it. You can be as active or inactive as you like. But once you get that M6 under your belt, most find that they want to push on and do more.

Being a qualified Radio Ham is certainly one skill that every prepper should have. Not only will making Slim Jim's become a piece of cake but you will find that there are so many different antenna designs to play with. You never know, you may even invent your own!

The Go Bag

The purpose of a Go Bag is straight forward. In the event of a situation occurring and you need to get away from your home, your car or any other place, just grab the bag and go. You will then have everything to hand that you need to maintain comms without her members of your family or group.

So, you have a radio or two and you have programmed them. No matter whether you have gone the Ham or PMR route, you need to make sure you have got the equipment you need to make sure you don't get caught out should a situation occur.

For each radio, the following are a must.

Replacement Antenna
Portable Slim Jim
Spare Battery
Car Charger
Waterproof Bag
USB Cable
Mains Charger
Pencil & Notebook
Burner Phone (Cheap Cell Phone) and SIM adapters
Frequency Lists
List of important telephone numbers
Copy of Ham Licence

Copy of house insurance and other documents
USB Charger (If available)
Antenna Adapters
Para Cord
Pocket Knife
Screwdrivers
Electrical Tape
Amalgamating Tape
Zip Ties
Torch
Ziploc Freezer Bags
Silica Gel Packets

I'm sure you can think of extra things that are pertinent to your situation.

When putting your bag together it is well worth making an inventory list and putting it in one of the side pockets of your Go Bag. This can be referred to on a regular basis in order to ensure that everything you need is present. As with any bespoke item like this, you may find that some items are redundant or that you need something else. The above list isn't designed to be anything other than a guide to what may be helpful.

The Burner Phone is an item that surprises people. It is well worth having. In the event of a power outage taking down the cell system, you will find that the battery on a smart phone will rapidly deplete as it constantly searches for a signal. Remove the SIM from your smart phone and put it in the burner. That way, not only are you not displaying expensive phones to people at a time when looting may occur, but you are also protecting the battery life of your smart phone.

The radio Go Bag is not designed to be a standard Preppers Go Bag, which normally contains a variety of kit. It is more designed to keep all the radio kit together. Many Prepper groups have a radio officer who they expect to be able to supply comms for all members. If this is you, then it is definitely worth doing this.

You may find that your own personal Go Bag contains your personal Radio. But maybe allocate yourself one in the Radio Go Bag in case that you and your personal bag get separated.

As for what type of bag to use for this, there are various considerations to take into account. Do you want a nice smart military style rucksack, or would that perhaps indicate to people that you have something worth stealing?

Or maybe a simple holdall that you would use for your gym kit? The choice really is yours.

Perhaps a good compromise would be a standard everyday hold-all that contains EDC pouches. EDC = Every Day Carry. Check them out on eBay and Amazon. There are some excellent cheap Chinese ones available, they normally involve a 2-week delivery window but I have purchased a few and they are excellent. But if you don't mind paying the money, 5.11 and Maxpedition make some excellent kit. Well worth considering.

RAYNET

RAYNET is a volunteer organisation of Radio Hams in the UK who regularly assist at public events like point to point racing, charity walks etc. They use their radios to help marshal the people involved and assist with message traffic. This is only one side of the organisation though and the main reason they exist is to provide communications during times of emergency. The groups use the public events in order to run through their own procedures and keep the members up to speed with RAYNET ways of doing things.

There are groups throughout the UK who vary in ability but some are very good indeed and have some slick systems and equipment that you could learn from. If you do go the route of becoming a Radio Ham then I would suggest investigating your nearest group to see what you can glean in the way of information.

Emergency Procedures

The Listening Watch

A system that can be employed by members of your group during times where a situation may occur. A flexible system that can be changed to better suit your needs but an example is this.

Have a pre-arranged frequency.
At the top of each hour, monitor that frequency for 3 minutes.
At the top of every third hour, carry out a roll call,
Repeat until an agreed stand down.

You will need to make arrangements for peoples sleep patterns etc. So maybe just run the net during certain hours etc.

This is ideal in times of likely bad weather, for instance flooding or storm force winds.

By only monitoring for 3 minutes at the top of the hour, you are ensuring that battery life is maintained at that people focus on comms as a priority for a short period. This soon becomes habit forming.

It should be noted that as a Radio Ham you are expected to be using your issued callsigns during communications. On PMR radios you can use whatever system of identification you like.

The Call Down System

It is quite possible that a situation arises out of the blue and no reasonable notice could be given of initiating a watch.

The call down works by having a cascade system on paper that everyone can use and refer to.

For example. Person A calls persons B and C. B calls D and E. C calls F and G and so on. Rapidly, a whole group of people can be alerted. Should someone not answer, the person who is calling them then takes responsibility for calling the people that the missing person would have called.

This makes it a guaranteed system. It can work using a telephone call or even text messaging.

If using text though you must ensure that a reply is received to ensure the person has been alerted.

The best part of this system is that anyone can initiate it. So, if person G decides to initiate, they assume the role of calling person A who then continues the system downward. With the added bonus that person C would call G to warn them, giving confidence that all was going to plan.

The system is fairly self-explanatory.

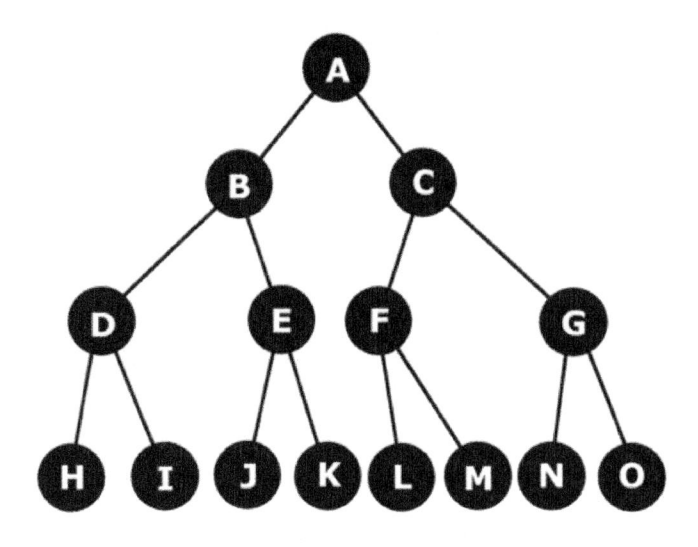

As the calldown is progressed, there needs to be an action to carry out. For instance, that a listening watch is in place at a certain frequency beginning with at a specified time. When this time comes, whoever is in charge of the net will do a check of who is listening and will keep a log. This is also the time that an explanation of the circumstances will be given and what the expectation of the members is.

EMP Hardening

EMP or Electromagnetic Pulse is a high voltage energy wave that can destroy electronics. There are several methods of causing EMP's. Some of them should be of concern to you from a health perspective, others purely from an electronics perspective. We will look at one way of protecting equipment from an EMP.

Causes of EMP

ICME. Interplanetary Coronal Mass Ejection

This is an event where the Sun ejects plasma and a magnetic field from the solar corona. You can imagine this as the Sun firing off electrical bullets if you like.

It happens regularly but due to the size of the sun and the different directions, they rarely come in our direction. It was once described to me as a man standing in the middle of a football field. he is spinning round whilst blindfolded and occasionally firing a pistol. The upshot of this is that someone is going to get hit one day.

When this CME hits the Earth, it creates reactions on both the day and night side. When these differences balance out, a large reaction occurs which causes a generation of power that can disrupt electronics.

Household Devices

Energy can be released at levels that interfere with radio and other electronic devices. An example is arcing within thermostats. The spark generates electrical interference.

NEMP. Nuclear Electromagnetic Pulse

An EMP generated by the detonation, normally at altitude, of a nuclear weapon. The detonation at height, causes a reaction in the Magnetosphere. Often seen as a pre-emptive strike weapon, NEMP can be used to take down a country or countries in a region and could have the effect of putting them back in the age of pre-technology. The EMP of a nuclear detonation is a secondary effect to the blast and other destructive abilities.

NNEMP. Non-Nuclear Electromagnetic Pulse

Sometimes referred to as E-Bombs. Created by a specific type of weapon which was developed to disrupt electrical systems. The effect of this weapons is suspected to be much smaller than that of nuclear devices and as such can be theoretically used to target smaller specific areas.

MEMP. Meteoric Electromagnetic Pulse

Caused by the entrance to the atmosphere of a meteor or other non-earthly body. The subsequent Electromagnetic discharge will cause disruption to electrical systems.

Lightning

A natural event that can wreck radios and other electronic devices. Caused by the arcing of a large electromagnetic pulse and followed by a train of smaller pulses which decrease over a rapid timeframe. Radio hams are known for disconnecting their antennas during thunderstorms.

The effects of EMP

An EMP has the effect of inducing a large amount of energy into power lines and devices containing electronic circuits. The energy overwhelms the fragile components and kills the devices. In power lines the resultant energy can be so high as to literally melt the lines off of the grid.
Transformers would fail and there no ready replacements as they are manufactured to order.

An EMP event could cause Nuclear Power Stations to fail over time as fail-safe devices begin to malfunction. This could result in catastrophic loss of control as seen in Chernobyl and Fukushima.

As mentioned earlier, if the EMP is caused by nuclear detonation, this effect is secondary. The resultant fireball is likely to ruin your day. Combined with the radioactive fallout, you may not be so worried about your radio.

Long the domain of Prepper lore, EMP is something that should not be ignored. In May 2017, various media sources reported that North Korea were working on EMP weapons and that the US may be a target. Whilst assessments may vary about the ability to deliver such a device, the fact is that people are waking up to the phenomena and how it would adversely affect society.

Preparation for EMP

It is possible to harden devices against the effects of EMP. For instance, a car can be placed in a shipping container. Radios and other electronics can be placed in smaller protective places.

The idea of doing this is not new. In the 1800's Michael Faraday invented a device which was named in his stead. The Faraday Cage has interesting protective qualities. The design of the Faraday Cage allows the effects of EMP to remain on the outside of the cage, washing past the fragile items inside. Compare it to standing on a rock when the tide comes in.

Without going into great technical detail, there are some simple ways that the normal person can protect Radio equipment. Of course, you could protect your expensive iPhones too, but without a cellular telephone system to use it on, you have a rather nice touch screen iPod.

As described, a Faraday Cage allows the energy to wash past the devices in the middle. Let's look at a simple Faraday Cage that you can make at home.

Make A Faraday Cage

If you are like many people in the UK, you may just have an empty or half eaten tin of chocolates left over from Christmas. The tight-fitting lids are perfect for use in a Faraday Cage.

Line the inside of the tin with cardboard. It is vitally important that items inside the 'cage' cannot actually touch the exterior metal.

Make sure that the lid is a tight fit. It must be able to conduct electricity across the main body of the tin and the lid. Consider using some sandpaper to remove paint and other detritus from the points where the two touch. Any gaps at all will render the cage useless.

Depending on what you want to protect, you may want to go bigger or smaller. I have seen metal dustbins lined with cardboard, lino and carpet. The idea is just the same.

If you don't have a tin, a cardboard box will suffice. You have to cover it in three layers of tinfoil to make it work. Test it out by putting a mobile phone inside and ringing it. You shouldn't get through. If you do, you need to work out where you have gone wrong. There are lots of designs for faraday cages on the internet.

Just remember, it's not just for disasters. You can use one of these to protect your equipment during an electricity storm.

Glossary of Terms

Aerial	Length of metal or wire connector to a radio to enable to the reception and transmission of radio signals.
Airband	Set of frequencies used by aircraft.
AM	Amplitude Modulation.
Amplifier	Electrical circuit that takes a small signal and increases it.
Antenna	See aerial.
Attenuation	The ability to reduce a signal that enters a radio. To prevent strong signals swamping a device.
Battery	Portable power supply.
Coax	See feeder.
Connector	An item that enables a cable to join a device.
Feeder	Cable that runs between a radio and an antenna.
Ferrite	Solid device that clips to a cable to prevent radio interference.

FM	Frequency Modulation.
Go Bag	A pre-prepared bag containing the equipment you need. Just grab and go.
Ham	Colloquial term for Amateur Radio.
Hertz	One cycle.
LSB	Lower Side Band.
Marine Band	Group of frequencies used by boats, ships and coastguard
Microphone	Converts sound into an electrical signal.
Plug	An electrical connector.
Radio	Device for transmitting or receiving a radio frequency signal
Speaker	Device that turns an electrical signal into sound.
SSB	Single Side Band.
UHF	Ultra-High Frequency.
USB	Upper Side Band.
VHF	Very High Frequency.
Watt	Unit of power.

Frequency Tables

PMR

Channel Name	Frequency	Mode
Analogue PMR		
UK Channel 1	446.00625	Narrow FM
UK Channel 2	446.01875	Narrow FM
UK Channel 3	446.03125	Narrow FM
UK Channel 4	446.04375	Narrow FM
UK Channel 5	446.05625	Narrow FM
UK Channel 6	446.06875	Narrow FM
UK Channel 7	446.08125	Narrow FM
UK Channel 8	446.09375	Narrow FM
Digital PMR		

UK Channel 1	446.103125	Digital
UK Channel 2	446.109375	Digital
UK Channel 3	446.115625	Digital
UK Channel 4	446.121875	Digital
UK Channel 5	446.128125	Digital
UK Channel 6	446.134375	Digital
UK Channel 7	446.140625	Digital
UK Channel 8	446.146875	Digital
UK Channel 9	446.153125	Digital
UK Channel 10	446.159375	Digital
UK Channel 11	446.165625	Digital
UK Channel 12	446.171875	Digital
UK Channel 13	446.178125	Digital
UK Channel 14	446.184375	Digital
UK Channel 15	446.190625	Digital
UK Channel 16	446.196875	Digital

Citizens Band (CB)

10KHz Channel spacing. You will notice the frequencies for the UK are completely sequential, the frequencies for the EU/CEPT channels are not. This isn't a typo.

Channel 9 is for distress
Channels 14 & 19 are for calling

Channel Name	UK Frequency	EU Frequency
1	27.60125	26.965
2	27.61125	26.975
3	27.62125	26.985
4	27.63125	27.005
5	27.64125	27.015
6	27.65125	27.025
7	27.66125	27.035
8	27.67125	27.055
9	27.68125	27.065
10	27.69125	27.075

11	27.70125	27.085
12	27.71125	27.105
13	27.72125	27.115
14	27.73125	27.125
15	27.74125	27.135
16	27.75125	27.155
17	27.76125	27.165
18	27.77125	27.175
19	27.78125	27.185
20	27.79125	27.205
21	27.80125	27.215
22	27.81125	27.225
23	27.82125	27.255
24	27.83125	27.235
25	27.84125	27.245
26	27.85125	27.265
27	27.86125	27.275
28	27.87125	27.285
29	27.88125	27.295
30	27.89125	27.305

31	27.90125	27.315
32	27.91125	27.325
33	27.92125	27.335
34	27.93125	27.345
35	27.94125	27.355
36	27.95125	27.365
37	27.96125	27.375
38	27.97125	27.385
39	27.98125	27.395
40	27.99125	27.405

Ham

I have listed the channelised frequencies of the 2 Metre and 70CM Ham bands here in the UK. Channels beginning "RV", "RU" and "RB" should never be used for anything other than accessing repeaters.

The simplex channels have changed in the past few years and this has led to renaming. The new naming system hasn't really caught on with Hams and you will often hear the old ones being used.

The change was caused by a change in channel spacing from 25KHz to 12.5KHz, doubling the number of available channels.

The new naming system is 'V', the old is 'S'.

RAYNET channels are for use by the RAYNET emergency teams only and should not be transmitted upon.

APRS is a Ham Radio packet data system frequency, do not transmit on it unless you are transmitting data packets designed for the APRS system.

2 Metre Band

Name	Frequency	Purpose
RV48	145.0000	Repeater Input
RV49	145.0125	Repeater Input
RV50	145.0250	Repeater Input
RV51	145.0375	Repeater Input
RV52	145.0500	Repeater Input
RV53	145.0625	Repeater Input
RV54	145.0775	Repeater Input
RV55	145.0875	Repeater Input
RV56	145.1000	Repeater Input
RV57	145.1125	Repeater Input
RV58	145.1250	Repeater Input
RV59	145.1375	Repeater Input
RV60	145.1500	Repeater Input
RV61	145.1625	Repeater Input
RV62	145.1750	Repeater Input
RV63	145.1875	Repeater Input

RAYNET 21	144.6250	RAYNET
RAYNET 22	144.6375	RAYNET
RAYNET 23	144.6500	RAYNET
RAYNET 24	144.6625	RAYNET
RAYNET 25	144.6750	RAYNET
RAYNET 26	144.7750	RAYNET
RAYNET 27	144.7875	RAYNET
RAYNET 28	144.8000	APRS (DATA)
RAYNET 29	144.8750	RAYNET
V16 (S8)	145.2000	RAYNET
V17	145.2125	Internet Gateway
V18 (S9)	145.2250	RAYNET
V19	145.2375	Internet Gateway
V20 (S10)	145.2500	Morse Practice

V21	145.2625	
V22 (S11)	145.2750	
V23	145.2875	
V24 (S12)	145.3000	
V25	145.3125	
V26 (S13)	145.3250	
V27	145.3375	
V28 (S14)	145.3500	
V29	145.3625	
V30 (S15)	145.3750	
V31	145.3875	
V32 (S16)	145.4000	
V33	145.4125	
V34 (S17)	145.4250	
V35	145.4375	
V36 (S18)	145.4500	
V37	145.4625	
V38 (S19)	145.4750	
V39	145.4875	
V40 (S20)	145.5000	Calling Channel

V41	145.5125	
V42 (S21)	145.5250	
V43	145.5375	
V44 (S22)	145.5500	
V45	145.5625	
V46	145.5750	
V47	145.5875	
RV48	145.6000	
RV49	145.6125	
RV50	145.6250	
RV51	145.6375	
RV52	145.6500	
RV53	145.6625	
RV54	145.6750	
RV55	145.6875	
RV56	145.7000	
RV57	145.7125	
RV58	145.7250	
RV59	145.7375	
RV60	145.7500	

RV61	145.7625	
RV62	145.7750	
RV63	145.7875	
ISS	145.8000	SPACE STATION

70CM Band

Name	Frequency	Purpose
U272 (SU16)	433.4000	Simplex Comms
U274 (SU17)	433.4250	Simplex Comms
U276 (SU18)	433.4500	Simplex Comms
U278 (SU19)	433.4750	Simplex Comms
U280 (SU20)	433.5000	Calling Channel
U282 (SU21)	433.5250	Simplex Comms
U284 (SU22)	433.5500	Simplex Comms
U286 (SU23)	433.5750	Simplex Comms
RAYNET 71	433.7000	Main Channel
RAYNET 72	433.7250	Second

		Channel
RAYNET 73	433.7500	Third Channel
RAYNET 74	433.7750	Reserve Channel
RAYNET 75	438.8125	
RAYNET 76	438.8250	
RAYNET 77	438.8375	
RAYNET 78	438.8500	
RAYNET 79	438.8625	
RAYNET 80	438.8750	
RAYNET 81	438.8875	
RAYNET 82	438.9000	
RAYNET 83	438.9125	
RAYNET 84A	438.4000	Repeater Output
RAYNET 84B	430.8000	Repeater Input
RU66	430.8250	Repeater Input
RU67	430.8375	Repeater Input
RU68	430.8500	Repeater Input
RU69	430.8625	Repeater Input

RU70	430.8750	Repeater Input
RU71	430.8875	Repeater Input
RU72	430.9000	Repeater Input
RU73	430.9125	Repeater Input
RU74	430.9250	Repeater Input
RU75	430.9375	Repeater Input
RU76	430.9500	Repeater Input
RU77	430.9625	Repeater Input
RU78	430.9750	Repeater Input
RB0	433.0000	Repeater Input
RB1	433.0250	Repeater Input
RB2	433.0500	Repeater Input
RB3	433.0750	Repeater Input
RB4	433.1000	Repeater Input
RB5	433.1250	Repeater Input
RB6	433.1500	Repeater Input
RB7	433.1750	Repeater Input
RB8	433.2000	Repeater Input
RB9	433.2250	Repeater Input

RB10	433.2500	Repeater Input
RB11	433.2750	Repeater Input
RB12	433.3000	Repeater Input
RB13	433.3250	Repeater Input
RB14	433.3500	Repeater Input
RB15	433.3750	Repeater Input
RU66	438.4250	Repeater Output
RU67	438.4375	Repeater Output
RU68	438.4500	Repeater Output
RU69	438.4625	Repeater Output
RU70	438.4750	Repeater Output
RU71	438.4875	Repeater Output
RU72	438.5000	Repeater Output
RU73	438.5125	Repeater Output

RU74	438.5250	Repeater Output
RU75	438.5375	Repeater Output
RU76	438.5500	Repeater Output
RU77	438.5625	Repeater Output
RU78	438.5750	Repeater Output
RB0	434.6000	Repeater Output
RB1	434.6250	Repeater Output
RB2	434.6500	Repeater Output
RB3	434.6750	Repeater Output
RB4	434.7000	Repeater Output
RB5	434.7250	Repeater Output
RB6	434.7500	Repeater Output

RB7	434.7750	Repeater Output
RB8	434.8000	Repeater Output
RB9	434.8250	Repeater Output
RB10	434.8500	Repeater Output
RB11	434.8750	Repeater Output
RB12	434.9000	Repeater Output
RB13	434.9250	Repeater Output
RB14	434.9500	Repeater Output
RB15	434.9750	Repeater Output

Marine Band

FM Channels as used in the UK. US and International frequencies are similar but may have different purposes. All channels are narrowband FM 12.5KHz.

Ch.	Simplex	Duplex	Purpose
0	156.000	X	UK HM Coastguard
1	156.050	160.650	
2	156.100	160.700	
3	156.150	160.750	
4	156.200	160.800	
5	156.250	160.850	
6	156.300	X	
7	156.350	160.950	
8	156.400	X	
9	156.450	X	
10	156.500	X	
11	156.550	X	
12	156.600	X	
13	156.650	X	

14	156.700	X	
15	156.750	X	
16	156.800	X	Distress, Safety and Calling
17	156.850	X	
18	156.900	161.500	
19	156.950	161.550	
20	157.000	161.600	
21	157.050	161.650	
22	157.100	161.700	
23	157.150	161.750	
24	157.200	161.800	
25	157.250	161.850	
26	157.300	161.900	
27	157.350	161.950	
28	157.400	162.000	
29	157.450	162.050	
30	157.500	162.100	
31	157.550	162.150	
32	157.600	162.200	
33	157.650	X	
34	157.700	162.300	

35	157.750	162.350	
36	157.800	162.400	
37	157.850	X	UK Marinas and Yacht Clubs
38	157.900	X	
39	157.950	162.550	
40	158.000	162.600	
41	158.050	162.650	
42	158.100	162.700	
43	158.150	162.750	
44	158.200	162.800	
45	158.250	162.850	
46	158.300	162.900	
47	158.350	162.950	
48	158.400	163.000	
49	158.450	X	
50	158.500	X	
51	158.550	X	
52	158.600	X	
53	158.650	X	
54	158.700	X	
55	158.750	X	

56	158.800	X	
57	158.850	X	
58	158.900	X	
59	158.950	X	
60	156.025	160.625	
61	156.075	160.675	
62	156.125	160.725	
63	156.175	160.775	
64	156.225	160.825	
65	156.275	160.875	
66	156.325	160.925	
67	156.375	X	UK Coastguard
68	156.425	X	
69	156.475	X	
70	156.525	X	Digital Selective Calling (DSC)
71	156.575	X	
72	156.625	X	
73	156.675	X	
74	156.725	X	
75	156.775	X	
76	156.825	X	

77	156.875	X	
78	156.925	161.525	
79	156.975	161.575	
80	157.025	161.625	UK Marinas
81	157.075	161.675	
82	157.125	161.725	
83	157.175	161.775	
84	157.225	161.825	
85	157.275	161.875	
86	157.325	161.925	
87	157.375	161.975	
88	157.425	162.025	
89	157.475	162.075	
90	157.525	162.125	
91	157.575	162.175	
92	157.625	162.225	
93	157.675	162.275	
94	157.725	162.325	
95	157.775	162.375	
96	157.825	162.425	
97	157.875	162.475	
98	157.925	162.525	

99	162.600	X	
100	158.025	162.625	
101	158.075	162.675	
102	158.125	162.725	
103	158.175	162.775	
104	158.225	162.825	
105	158.275	162.875	
106	158.325	162.925	
107	158.375	162.975	
108	158.425	X	
109	158.475	X	
M	157.850	X	UK Marinas and Yacht Clubs
M2	161.425	X	UK Marinas and Yacht Clubs
AIS 1	162.025	X	Automatic Identification System (data)
AIS 2	161.975	X	Automatic Identification System (data)

Air Band

I have included some frequencies here for interest. The Baofeng radio is capable of receiving these frequencies but you will not hear them properly as the Baofeng is FM only and these channels operate in AM.

Name	Frequency	Purpose
ECAS	121.5000	Emergency Communications and Aid Service
Depcom	122.9500	Helicopters at airfields with no ground radio facilities
Civil A2A	123.4500	Civil Air to Air Common
Safetycom	135.4750	Aircraft at airfields with no ground radio facilities
Helimed	166.4375	Emergency Reserve Channel
Eastern Radar	135.2750	
Eastern	299.9750	

Radar		
Eastern Radar	230.6000	
Eastern Radar	245.3250	
Eastern Radar	250.2750	
Eastern Radar	251.6250	
Eastern Radar	254.8250	
Eastern Radar	255.7000	
Eastern Radar	261.0000	
Eastern Radar	263.0750	
Eastern Radar	275.6750	
Eastern Radar	277.7750	
Eastern Radar	278.1500	

Eastern Radar	279.3000	
Eastern Radar	282.3000	
Eastern Radar	283.6750	
Eastern Radar	284.3000	
Eastern Radar	290.3000	
Eastern Radar	290.6000	
Eastern Radar	291.1750	
Eastern Radar	291.7750	
Eastern Radar	292.6000	
Eastern Radar	293.4750	
Eastern Radar	293.5250	
Eastern Radar	293.5750	

London ATCC	118.3750	
London ATCC	118.4750	
London ATCC	120.0250	
London ATCC	120.5250	
London ATCC	121.0250	
London ATCC	121.2750	
London ATCC	118.3750	
London ATCC	118.4750	
London ATCC	120.0250	
London ATCC	120.5250	
London ATCC	121.0250	
London ATCC	121.2750	

London ATCC	124.2750	
London ATCC	127.7000	
London ATCC	128.0500	
London ATCC	128.4250	
London ATCC	128.6250	
London ATCC	129.2000	
London ATCC	129.6000	
London ATCC	131.0500	
London ATCC	131.1250	
London ATCC	131.2000	
London ATCC	132.3000	
London ATCC	132.4500	

London ATCC	132.6000	
London ATCC	132.8000	
London ATCC	132.9500	
London ATCC	133.4500	
London ATCC	133.5250	
London ATCC	133.6000	
London ATCC	133.7000	
London ATCC	134.4250	
London ATCC	134.4500	
London ATCC	134.9000	
London ATCC	135.0500	
London ATCC	135.2500	

London ATCC	135.3250	
London ATCC	135.5250	
London ATCC	136.2750	
London ATCC	136.5500	
London TMA	118.8250	
London TMA	119.7750	
London TMA	120.1750	
London TMA	121.2250	
London TMA	121.3250	
London TMA	123.9000	
London TMA	125.8000	
London TMA	125.9000	
London TMA	126.3000	
London TMA	126.8750	
London TMA	127.4250	
London TMA	128.4000	
London TMA	129.2750	

London TMA	125.9500	
London TMA	126.3000	
London TMA	126.8750	
London TMA	127.4250	
London TMA	128.4000	
London TMA	129.2750	
London TMA	130.9250	
London TMA	132.0500	
London TMA	133.1750	
London TMA	133.9750	
London TMA	134.7500	
London TMA	135.5750	
London FIS	124.6000	
London FIS	124.7500	
London Mil	127.4500	
London Mil	128.2500	
London Mil	131.2250	
London Mil	133.3000	
London Mil	133.3250	

London Mil	133.9000	
London Mil	135.0750	
London Mil	135.1500	
London Mil	135.2750	
London Mil	135.9250	
London Mil	231.6250	
London Mil	231.9750	
London Mil	235.0500	
London Mil	244.3750	
London Mil	249.6250	
London Mil	249.6750	
London Mil	250.2750	
London Mil	251.6250	
London Mil	254.2250	
London Mil	254.9000	
London Mil	255.4000	
London Mil	257.2250	
London Mil	261.0250	
London Mil	262.9750	

London Mil	264.8250	
London Mil	268.9750	
London Mil	270.0000	
London Mil	275.4750	
London Mil	277.1250	
London Mil	277.9500	
London Mil	278.0250	
London Mil	279.1750	
London Mil	279.2250	
London Mil	279.4750	
London Mil	282.1250	
London Mil	283.5250	
London Mil	284.8750	
London Mil	285.1750	
London Mil	290.5750	
London Mil	290.7000	
London Mil	290.9250	
London Mil	291.8000	
London Mil	292.5250	

Scottish ATCC	119.8750	
Scottish ATCC	123.9750	
Scottish ATCC	124.0500	
Scottish ATCC	124.5000	
Scottish ATCC	125.6750	
Scottish ATCC	126.2500	
Scottish ATCC	126.8500	
Scottish ATCC	127.2750	
Scottish ATCC	129.2250	
Scottish ATCC	131.3000	
Scottish ATCC	133.2000	
Scottish ATCC	133.6750	

Scottish ATCC	133.8000
Scottish ATCC	134.7750
Scottish ATCC	135.6750
Scottish ATCC	135.8500
Scottish Mil	134.3000
Scottish Mil	134.4750
Scottish Mil	244.3250
Scottish Mil	249.4250
Scottish Mil	249.4750
Scottish Mil	249.5250
Scottish Mil	252.4750
Scottish Mil	255.7750
Scottish Mil	258.0000
Scottish Mil	259.1750
Scottish Mil	259.7250
Scottish Mil	259.7750
Scottish Mil	268.2500

Scottish Mil	268.9250	
Scottish Mil	285.0750	
Scottish Mil	292.6750	
Shanwick Radar	123.9500	
Shanwick Radar	127.6500	
Shanwick Radar	135.5250	
Heathrow Approach	119.5000	
Heathrow Approach	119.7250	
Heathrow Approach	134.9750	
Heathrow Approach	135.1250	
Heathrow Approach	127.5500	
Heathrow Radar	119.2000	
Heathrow Radar	119.5000	

Heathrow Radar	119.9000	
Heathrow Radar	120.4000	
Heathrow Radar	127.5500	
Heathrow Tower	118.7000	
Heathrow Tower	118.5000	
Heathrow Tower	124.4750	
Heathrow Clearance	121.9750	
Heathrow Ground	121.9000	
Gatwick Radar	126.8250	
Gatwick Radar	119.6000	
Gatwick Radar	118.9500	
Gatwick Radar	134.2250	

| Gatwick Tower | 124.2250 | |
| Gatwick Ground | 121.8000 | |

Phonetic Alphabet

A – Alpha
B – Bravo
C – Charlie
D – Echo
F – Foxtrot
G – Golf
H – Hotel
I – India
J – Juliet
K – Kilo
L – Lima
M – Mike
N – November
O – Oscar
P – Papa
Q – Quebec
R – Romeo
S – Sierra
T – Tango
U – Uniform
V – Victor
W – Whiskey
X – X-ray
Y – Yankee
Z – Zulu

Morse Code

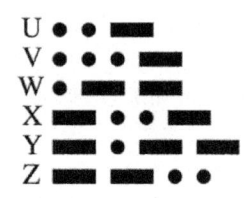

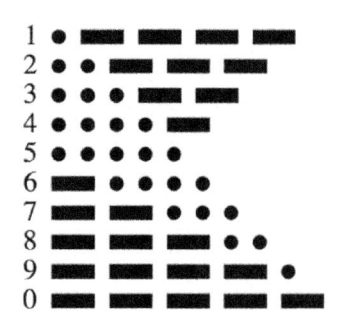

A ●▬
B ▬●●●
C ▬●▬●
D ▬●●
E ●
F ●●▬●
G ▬▬●
H ●●●●
I ●●
J ●▬▬▬
K ▬●▬
L ●▬●●
M ▬▬
N ▬●
O ▬▬▬
P ●▬▬●
Q ▬▬●▬
R ●▬●
S ●●●
T ▬

U ●●▬
V ●●●▬
W ●▬▬
X ▬●●▬
Y ▬●▬▬
Z ▬▬●●

1 ●▬▬▬▬
2 ●●▬▬▬
3 ●●●▬▬
4 ●●●●▬
5 ●●●●●
6 ▬●●●●
7 ▬▬●●●
8 ▬▬▬●●
9 ▬▬▬▬●
0 ▬▬▬▬▬

Contact

Thank you for purchasing this book. If you notice any errors or have suggestions about how it can be improved, I would love to hear from you.

Please email me:
prepcommsuk@gmail.com

Ham Radio Training

START YOUR AMATEUR RADIO JOURNEY

WITH "FOUNDATION ONLINE"

If you're looking to get your Amateur Radio Foundation Licence, then you can take the hassle out of studying with our online amateur radio training course:

- ✓ Study at your leisure
- ✓ Video Tutorials
- ✓ Online presentations
- ✓ Mock tests
- ✓ Monthly courses

And the cost? **Free!**

Our online course teaches the entire Foundation syllabus in short modules, each with a short revision quiz to aid learning. The course runs in an online classroom, with lessons delivered over three weeks. At the end, our mock test gives you an idea whether you'd be likely to pass before you commit to the Foundation exam.

Sign up to **"Foundation Online"** today, and start your journey...

www.hamtrain.co.uk

Printed in Dunstable, United Kingdom